S0-CFL-672

Straight Talk About Betrayal

Straight Talk

About

Betrayal

*A Self-Help
Guide
for Couples*

DONNA R. BELLAFIORE, LCSW, CADC

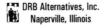

DRB Alternatives, Inc.
Naperville, Illinois

Book design:
MarketWrite
Services, Inc.

All rights reserved. Printed in the
United States of America. No part of
this publication may be reproduced or
transmitted in any form or by any
means, electronic or mechanical,
including photocopy, recording, or any
information storage and retrieval
system, without permission in writing
from the publisher.

Copyright © 1999 by Donna R.
Bellafiore

Published in 1999 in the United States
of America by DRB Alternatives, Inc.,
608 S. Washington Street, Naperville,
Illinois 60540.

ISBN: 0-9668759-0-7

To my husband, my friend, who supports everything I do. To my son, who inspires me to meet challenges. To my daughter, who shares my spirit and my dreams. To other family members and friends, who never fail to cheer me.

Contents

Contents
(con't.)

Acknowledgments

I wish to thank all of the people I know personally and professionally who have generously shared their stories and their pain. Thank you, Carol Heil, my editor, for understanding me and for becoming my friend. Thank you, too, Suzanne Hlotke and *The Chicago Tribune* and *Copley Newspapers* for helping make my book a reality.

When cheated,
wife or husband
feels the same.

EURIPIDES
c. 426 B.C.

Straight Talk

Since earliest times, married and unmarried couples have felt the devastation of a partner's unfaithfulness. Betrayal, in any form, kills trust and inflicts pain and feelings of loss not unlike those experienced upon death.

Grief and recovery

In truth, when a partner's unfaithfulness is discovered or revealed, a relationship—weak or strong—dies. How well partners work through grief and survive or "rebuild" depends on their commitment to each other and the relationship, their levels of tolerance for pain, the ability to understand their own and each other's needs, and the kinds of comfort and unbiased support available to them.

Grief Is Not...

Grief is not a mountain to be climbed, with the strong reaching the summit long before the weak.

Grief is not an athletic event, with stop watches timing our progress.

Grief is a walk through loss and pain with no competition and no time trials.

AUTHOR UNKNOWN

Infidelity must be faced openly to initiate recovery.

Recovery as a process

Once a closely held secret or, at best, a whisper to be swept under rugs, infidelity is a painful reality that must be faced openly to initiate recovery. The process has several stages which unfold slowly. These stages are not defined by clear boundaries, nor does everyone move through them sequentially.

Navigating turbulence

Recovery is like being swept into a swollen river after a storm. Each partner struggles with mixed emotions. Forces may at times push partners together, at other times, apart. Even in calm spots, partners must work to remain afloat and recover.

Emotional snags

It's not uncommon for relationships to end before the process of recovery is complete. One or both partners may get hung up along the "river." Intense anger and hurt may block their ability to break free and move forward.

Relational ties and recovery

Sometimes, to escape the natural flow, partners cling to their earlier promise or commitment like a tree branch, only to find it's too weak to bear the weight of their emotions. The relationship breaks prematurely because it lacked the vitality and strength needed to support both partners through the full recovery process.

Recovery *for the Hurt Partner*

The process has several stages which unfold slowly.

Hurt Partner

1. Emotional and intellectual shock. Questioning of reality. Relief if suspicions have been confirmed. Intense emotional pain.

2. Humiliation and anger. Blaming. Desire for retaliation, revenge. May reject partner's touch, finding physical contact intolerable. Or, may engage in "bargaining behavior" to save relationship.

3. Obsession or preoccupation with the affair.

4. Feelings of shame, isolation, rejection, and grief. May be accompanied by depression, overwhelming sadness, and physical aches.

5. Acceptance and increased ability to talk about the betrayal with less intensity.

6. Reexamination and evaluation of the relationship.

7. Decision to rebuild and strengthen the relationship or to separate.

Recovery *for the Unfaithful Partner*

These stages are not defined by clear boundaries, nor does everyone move through them sequentially.

Unfaithful Partner

1. Desire for reconciliation and forgiveness. May co-exist with relief that secret is out, or regret that affair is over. If affair was exposed by another individual(s), may feel anger toward that person(s).

2. Emotional and physical withdrawal. Desire to forget.

3. Anger and resentment when partner discusses the affair. May feel defensive and blame partner, upbringing, or society for the betrayal.

4. Confusion, shame, sadness. Sense of guilt or, less often, distress over lack of guilty feelings. Ambivalence and uncertainty about real reasons for unfaithfulness.

5. Acknowledgment of hurtful behavior and personal pain.

6. Reexamination and evaluation of the relationship.

7. Decision to rebuild and strengthen the relationship or to separate.

Practical Steps

Time is betrayal's great healer, but practical steps and a strong support system can advance healing in both partners.

Seek practical steps and a strong support system to promote your personal health and healing.

For the Hurt Partner:

Preserving health and energy

Grieving the loss of what you believed to be a trusting relationship, your need for rest and reassurance is great. It's very important that you take care of yourself. Not eating or sleeping will only deplete energy needed for your recovery.

Emotional composure

Flooded with emotions in the earliest days, you may find it nearly impossible to speak as your usual self. You may feel as if you're riding a roller coaster, fearing you're going to scream, cry, or "explode" whenever you speak.

Anger

Angry outbursts will only turn your partner away by tapping into his or her vulnerabilities. Your partner's defenses will then go up, and he or she may not be able to listen, let alone, respond.

Consider seriously whether you want your partner to hear you at this time. Can you speak without blame or criticism that will cause him or her to withdraw? Can you contain your very real and understandable anger

Avoid angry outbursts which can cause your partner to become defensive.

and the overwhelming desire to scream?

Seek a safe environment where you can divulge your "secret."

Personal support systems

Healthful venting is difficult, but essential, to your recovery. You need to find a safe environment where you can divulge your "secret" and express emotions candidly. Speaking to a trusted and supportive friend or family member may be helpful. Or, you may want to seek counsel from a spiritual leader or trained professional.

Exercise and healthful activities

Exercise will help you release the stress and strain of your emotions. So may therapeutic massage. Journaling may be help-

ful, allowing you to express your
feelings in writing before speaking
with your partner about them.

Positive messaging
   When you speak to your
partner, avoid "you" messages:
      "You lied!"
      "You betrayed me!"
      "You've destroyed us!"
      "How could you do this to
         me?"

   Speak, instead, of your pain
using "I" language:
      "I'm hurt."
      "What hurts me most is not
         understanding how this
         happened."
      "This is so painful, because I

**Speak of your
pain using "I"
language: "I'm
hurt."**

thought our partnership was built on trust."

Repeat or paraphrase statements to keep conversation flowing with your partner.

"*I*" statements that focus on pain, instead of blame, will open the door to positive communication. They must, too, be accompanied by your willingness to listen. Demonstrate openness to your partner's explanation by looking at him or her while you're listening.

Paraphrasing

Repeat or paraphrase statements to keep the conversation going. For example, if your partner says, "I had the affair because you were too busy. I just wasn't getting enough attention," you might respond, "You felt I was too busy and didn't give you enough attention. Is that right? Is there anything more?"

Showing respect

If your goal, at this point, is to stay in your relationship, you must treat your partner with respect. This increases the likelihood that he or she will perceive and mirror your behavior.

Recall how forces in the "river" drove you apart? When you now reach a calm place where you can come together and talk, you need to show mutual respect for each other to navigate rough spots ahead.

Claiming your role

Resist immediate temptation to assume self-blame for what has happened; rather, take time for honest reflection. Prior to the affair, did your partner try to speak with you about problems in your relationship? If so, did you listen or discount the appeal?

Not all partners directly communicate thoughts and feelings about their needs. Self-reflection will help you determine how active or passive your role may have been in circumstances leading up to the breach. As you reflect, you must consider whether you can or want to invest the energy it takes to improve communication and chart a new course for your partnership.

Take time for honest reflection.

Self-reflection will help you determine how active or passive your role may have been in circumstances leading up to the breach.

"Bargaining"

During the recovery period, many hurt partners engage in "bargaining behavior." Self-esteem diminished, they try to save the relationship at any cost.

Avoid "bargaining," which may erode your self-esteem and offer a false sense of improvement in your relationship.

If, at heart, you blame yourself for the infidelity and decide it's all within your power to make things better, you may find yourself doing things you wouldn't ordinarily do. If so, you're "bargaining" for approval from your partner.

Try to recognize atypical behavior—behaving in ways that are not true to yourself—because "bargaining" may further erode your self-esteem and offer a false sense of improvement in your relationship.

Preoccupation/obsession

Your recovery, too, may include a period of preoccupation with the betrayal. You may dream about your partner "in the act," or you may, fully awake, visualize over and over the circumstances of his or her betrayal.

Disengaging

Preoccupation is a common, but unhealthy, phase of recovery. A practical way to move forward is through "STOP" behavior. Whenever you become conscious of another "replay," you must tell yourself, literally, to "STOP!" The self-imposed check, when ob-

served, will help disengage you
from more hurtful obsession.

Limiting "recovery talk"

Similarly, a "contract" with
your partner which sets time limits
for discussion will help you
maintain balance and energy for
recovery. Some couples agree to
ten minutes a day for "recovery
talk"; others accept thirty minutes
or less, once a week.

The amount of time agreed
upon is less important than showing mutual respect for the limit.
Too often, communication breaks
down because the hurt partner
finds it difficult to stop talking
about the betrayal.

*Set and observe a
time limit for
discussions to
help maintain
balance and en-
ergy for recovery.*

Support groups

Throughout your recovery, you will need considerable support. In some communities, support groups for betrayed partners exist. Advantages of such groups include recognition that you are not alone in your suffering and opportunities to gain from others' experiences. Look for notices in your local newspaper.

Reading

Articles and books dealing with the pain of infidelity may also provide comfort. A list of recommended titles appears on page 31.

Examining relationship

As you recover and your self-esteem improves, you'll be able to examine your relationship more closely. If your partner has been able to share his or her pain and the reasons for being unfaithful, you may reflect on underlying causes and unfulfilled needs. Determining whether you can, or wish to, meet these needs—and whether your partner can, and wishes to, meet yours—will take time and serious consideration.

Reflect honestly on your relationship.

The tear-out section of this book (starting on pg. 35) poses questions that will help you clarify feelings about your relationship.

Addictions

Your best efforts and desire to mend the relationship quickly may be thwarted if your partner is addicted to alcohol, drugs, sex, or gambling. Addictions are powerful conditions that require knowledge and intervention. Without them, recurrence of infidelity is always possible, and your desire for a healthy, balanced relationship can't be realized.

Decisions

Even without addictions, decisions about the future will be complicated. You may be experiencing emotional or physical abuse. Your financial situation may be unstable. Your partner, at the same time, may be a good parent to your children. You may feel committed to him or her for religious reasons. Or, you may be deeply in love.

Ultimately, you must decide whether to rebuild or dissolve the relationship. Your final choice can happen independently, or you and your partner can come to a mutual agreement. Either way, try to approach your decision with as much inner strength and clarity of thought as possible, for infidelity issues are as complex as the partnership itself.

Personal growth

Relationships enrich the human experience, and despite their risks, will always be part of your life. If you take what learning you can from this painful interlude, you'll grow in your ability to establish and maintain more satisfying relationships in the future.

Take what learning you can from this painful interlude to grow in your ability to establish and maintain more satisfying relationships in the future.

For the Unfaithful Partner:

Confused feelings

At the moment, you may be carrying a burden of mixed emotions. You may feel sorry that the affair happened...sad that it ended...guilt over your behavior...or entitled...perhaps even justified. You may resent your partner and feel, at best, ambivalent about ending the affair.

If you developed serious feelings for the other person, you may feel a keen sense of loss. Repercussions of a long, emotionally-involved affair are quite different from those of a short-lived, low-intensity affair. The former incites significant personal and interpersonal pain, while the latter is more readily "forgotten."

Managing conflict

To manage conflicting feelings about your relationships, professional counseling may be beneficial. A professional can help you sort out myriad thoughts and feelings and help you understand your partner's vacillating emotions. He or she can also explore with you ways to manage conflict.

Consider professional counseling to help you sort out myriad thoughts and feelings and help you understand your partner's vacillating emotions.

Recovery challenges

Even with help, recovery may be slow and grueling. You have many decisions and adjustments to make if your partnership is to endure. At times, you may feel like "throwing your hands up" in frustration, because the relationship isn't mending quickly.

Explore new ways to nurture yourself, perhaps through exercise or therapeutic massage.

Patience

Patience and "going with the flow" will carry you a long ways down the "river." If patience doesn't come naturally, it can be learned. An effective, patience-building practice is to set sight on your long-term goal and work slowly, but actively, toward that vision.

Healthful activities

Reaching your goal demands taking care of yourself during recovery. Allow time to explore new ways to nurture yourself, perhaps through exercise or therapeutic massage. These and other healthful activities will help restore your sense of well-being and emotional balance.

Withdrawal

Balance may be challenged by a temptation to withdraw emotionally and physically from your partner. Withdrawal should be resolutely avoided, because it closes doors to the possibility of reconciliation.

Avoid emotional and physical withdrawal from your partner.

Honesty

Your partner may immediately ask for details of the affair. Despite personal embarrassment or discomfort, you should respond truthfully. Honest answers will validate your partner's pain and help facilitate his or her recovery.

Listen and empathize with your partner's feelings to bring the right balance of candor and restraint to the situation.

On the other hand, total "airing" of your infidelity may be harmful if your partner isn't emotionally ready to hear details of your unfaithfulness. You must listen and empathize with your partner's feelings to bring the right balance of candor and restraint to the situation.

Questions, questions

Seeking constant reassurance, your partner will eventually ask questions, even if probing (or "grilling") conflicts with your desire to move on. As trust is regained, the questions will diminish.

Partner's preoccupation

Before questioning ends,

however, your partner may go through a period of preoccupation with real or imagined circumstances of your affair. Observing this and having to account repeatedly for your behavior may tax your inner resources and increase your uncertainty about reconciliation.

Anticipate that your partner may experience a period of preoccupation with details of your affair.

Limiting discussion

A "contract" with your partner that sets time limits on discussions will help channel his or her thoughts and overwhelming need to "talk." At the same time, support and honest confessions during discussion periods can lead to acknowledgment and acceptance of your own and your partner's very real pain. This breakthrough will help you explore the causes for your infidelity and help determine whether or not the relationship can ultimately be restored.

Accept that your recovery will be unique.

New behaviors

Whatever the outcome, this is an ideal opportunity for you to establish new patterns of behavior to enhance, rather than harm, the emotional state of people you care about.

For Both Partners:

Unique recoveries

Just as individuals and partnerships are unique, so are recoveries. One or both of you may experience some or all stages of the process, in an orderly or random fashion.

What's important is knowing that there *is* a recovery process, and there *are* ways to manage conflict resulting from infidelity. Fortunately, more avenues of support exist today than ever before.

To promote recovery, don't hesitate to seek refuges of emotional support, as individuals and as a couple.

Emotional refuges

Finding refuges of emotional support—individually and as a couple—is vital to recovery. There, with self-reflection and the listening ear of a supportive friend or couple's counselor, you can experience personal growth by sharing not only the essence of your experience, but shades of dif-

ference that make your recovery
uniquely your own.

Reading List

Lusterman, Don-David. *Infidelity:
A Survival Guide.* Oakland, CA:
New Harbinger Publications,
Inc., 1998.

Pittman, Frank. *Private Lies: Infidelity
and Betrayal of Intimacy.* New
York: W.W. Norton & Co.,
1989.

Spring, Janis Abrahms with Mich-
ael Spring. *After the Affair: Healing the Pain and Rebuilding Trust
When a Partner Has Been Unfaithful.* New York: HarperCol-
lins, 1997.

Subotnik, Rona, and Gloria G.
Harris. *Surviving Infidelity:
Making Decisions, Recover-
ing from the Pain.* Holbrook,
MA: Bob Adams, Inc., 1994.

Voices *of Betrayal*

I'd say it's the worst thing I've ever had to go through.

How could she do this to me?

What I perceive from him is that he doesn't know half the stuff that's going on with me now.

Who is this person I'm living with?

I decided not to give up, even though it's real painful to see someone you love self-destruct. She could've taken my kids, and I couldn't do anything about it.

Will I ever be able to trust him again?

I'm full of suspicion, doubt, anger. But, he's in the mind-frame, "It's behind us. Let's go on."

How do I know if she's lying?

I'm so ashamed, I've told no one about this.

I am going to tell my children. Not any specifics, but I am going to talk to them and let them know if they are going to marry, it's a lifelong commitment. It's more than just "I love you. Will you marry me?" You have to stay true to that person.

Will I ever get over this feeling?

I'm hoping, now that our family's mood is calming down, she'll want to let go of her guilt and say she's sorry.

Did I do something wrong? Is there something wrong with me?

Exploring *your relationship*

*A Tear-Out
Section
for Couples*

Recovery *for Both Partners*

Hurt Partner	Unfaithful Partner
1. Emotional and intellectual shock. Questioning of reality. Relief if suspicions have been confirmed. Intense emotional pain.	1. Desire for reconciliation and forgiveness. May co-exist with relief that secret is out or regret that affair is over. If affair was exposed by another individual(s), may feel anger toward that person(s).
2. Humiliation and anger. Blaming. Desire for retaliation, revenge. May reject partner's touch, finding physical contact intolerable. Or, may engage in "bargaining behavior" to save relationship.	2. Emotional and physical withdrawal. Desire to forget.
3. Obsession or preoccupation with the affair.	3. Anger and resentment when partner discusses the affair. May feel defensive and blame partner, upbringing, or society for the betrayal.
4. Feelings of shame, isolation, rejection, and grief. May be accompanied by depression, overwhelming sadness, and physical aches.	4. Confusion, shame, sadness. Sense of guilt or, less often, distress over lack of guilty feelings. Ambivalence and uncertainty about real reasons for unfaithfulness.
5. Acceptance and increased ability to talk about the betrayal with less intensity.	5. Acknowledgment of hurtful behavior and personal pain.
6. Reexamination and evaluation of the relationship.	6. Reexamination and evaluation of the relationship.
7. Decision to rebuild and strengthen the relationship or to separate.	7. Decision to rebuild and strengthen the relationship or to separate.

Copyright © 1999 by Donna R. Bellafiore

Questions _for the Hurt Partner_

1. _How do I define a healthy relationship?_

2. _What does commitment mean to me?_

3. _Do I love my partner? Is love enough for me? Why or why not?_

4. _What qualities do I look for in a friend?_

5. _Do I/did I consider my partner my friend? Why or why not?_

6. _What traits first attracted me to my partner?_

7. *How has he or she changed?*

8. *How have I changed?*

9. *Have I been trying to change my partner? If so, in what way(s)?*

10. *Has my partner been trying to change me? If so, in what way(s)?*

11. *What behavior(s), if any, am I willing to change in myself?*

12. *Prior to this betrayal, was I happy in our relationship? Why or why not?*

13. *What are my beliefs about infidelity? How do they compare to my partner's beliefs?*

14. *What similarities do I find in this relationship and other unfulfilling ones, if any, I've experienced?*

15. *Do I harbor old resentments? Can I share these and other personal thoughts and feelings with my partner? Why or why not?*

16. *How well do my partner and I listen and respond to each other?*

17. *Do I believe our relationship can improve? Why or why not?*

18. Do I feel "stuck"? If so, for what reason(s)?

19. How important is "rebuilding" to me?

20. How willing am I to work towards improving our relationship? What if my partner isn't equally willing?

21. What is/are my fear(s) about the future?

22. Can I accept and live with whatever decision I make?

Strengths of my partnership	Weaknesses of my partnership
+	-
+	-
+	-

Questions *for the Unfaithful Partner*

1. *How do I define a healthy relationship?*

2. *What does commitment mean to me?*

3. *Do I love my partner? Is love enough for me? Why or why not?*

4. *What qualities do I look for in a friend?*

5. *Do I/did I consider my partner my friend? Why or why not?*

6. *What traits first attracted me to my partner?*

7. *How has he or she changed?*

8. *How have I changed?*

9. *Have I been trying to change my partner? If so, in what way(s)?*

10. *Has my partner been trying to change me? If so, in what way(s)?*

11. *What behavior(s), if any, am I willing to change in myself?*

12. *Prior to this betrayal, was I happy in our relationship? Why or why not?*

13. *What are my beliefs about infidelity? How do they compare to my partner's beliefs?*

14. *What similarities do I find in this relationship and other unfulfilling ones, if any, I've experienced?*

15. *Do I harbor old resentments? Can I share these and other personal thoughts and feelings with my partner? Why or why not?*

16. *How well do my partner and I listen and respond to each other?*

17. *Do I believe our relationship can improve? Why or why not?*

18. Do I feel "stuck"? If so, for what reason(s)?

19. How important is "rebuilding" to me?

20. How willing am I to work towards improving our relationship? What if my partner isn't equally willing?

21. What is/are my fear(s) about the future?

22. Can I accept and live with whatever decision I make?

Strengths of my partnership	Weaknesses of my partnership
+	-
+	-
+	-

Index

About the Author

I hope this brief overview of betrayal's complexities offers comfort and encouragement to couples who are beginning to explore pathways to recovery.

D. Bellafiore

DONNA R. BELLAFIORE is a licensed clinical social worker and therapist and a certified alcohol and other drug counselor who practices in Naperville, Illinois. Her compassionate counseling approaches, designed to help men and women overcome the pain of infidelity, are gaining national attention. *Beyond Betrayal*^{SM}, her professionally facilitated support groups, have been profiled in *The Chicago Tribune* and other media. Through DRB Alternatives, Inc., she provides telephone counseling and free self-support services on her electronic bulletin board at *www.tmg.net/drb*. Additional copies of her book are available through DRB Alternatives' Web site and many bookstores.